TAKE THE LEAD
CLARINET

Rock'n'Roll

Series Editor: Anna Joyce

Editorial, production and recording: Artemis Music Limited • Design and production: Space DPS Limited • Published 2000

IMP
International MUSIC Publications

Demonstration

Backing

Be-Bop-A-Lula

Words and Music by
Tex Davis and Gene Vincent

Demonstration

Backing

Blue Suede Shoes

Words and Music by Carl Lee Perkins

CODA

Blueberry Hill

Words and Music by Al Lewis,
Vincent Rose and Larry Stock

8

C'mon Everybody

Words and Music by
Jerry Capehart and Eddie Cochran

Demonstration

Backing

Great Balls Of Fire

Words and Music by
Jack Hammer and Otis Blackwell

Whatever your instrument is... you can

TAKE THE LEAD

The Take The Lead books are what aspiring solo performers have been holding their breath for!

If you want to take the lead, then these are the books for you.

• Each comes with a CD containing full backing tracks for the soloist to play along with, and demonstration tracks to help you learn the songs.

• Ideal for solo or ensemble use, since they are all arranged in the same concert pitch key.

• Each book includes carefully selected and edited top line arrangements; chord symbols in concert pitch.

A

Air That I Breathe, The	TTL - 90s Hits
Angels	TTL - 90s Hits

B

Bailamos	TTL - Latin
Be-Bop-A-Lula	TTL - Rock 'n' Roll
Because You Loved Me	TTL - Movie Hits
Believe	TTL - Number One Hits
Birdland	TTL - Jazz
Blue Monday	TTL - Movie Hits
Blue Suede Shoes	TTL - Rock 'n' Roll
Blueberry Hill	TTL - Rock 'n' Roll

C

Careless Whisper	TTL - Number One Hits
Chattanooga Choo Choo	TTL - Swing
Cherry Pink And Apple Blossom White	TTL - Latin
Choo Choo Ch'Boogie	TTL - Swing
C'mon Everybody	TTL - Rock 'n' Roll
Coronation Street	TTL - TV Themes
Christmas Song, The (Chestnuts Roasting On An Open Fire)	TTL - Christmas Songs

D

Dance Of The Sugar Plum Fairy from... The Nutcracker (Tchaikovsky)	TTL - Classical Collection
Dancing Queen	TTL - Number One Hits
	STL - Chart Hits
Desafinado	TTL - Jazz
Don't Get Around Much Anymore	TTL - Jazz

E

Everybody Needs Somebody To Love	TTL - The Blues Brothers
(Everything I Do) I Do It For You	TTL - Movie Hits

F

Fascinating Rhythm	TTL - Jazz
Flying Without Wings	TTL - Number One Hits
	STL - Chart Hits
Frosty The Snowman	TTL - Christmas Songs
Frozen	TTL - 90s Hits

G

Gimme Some Lovin'	TTL - The Blues Brothers
Great Balls Of Fire	TTL - Rock 'n' Roll
Green Door, The	TTL - Rock 'n' Roll
Guantanamera	TTL - Latin

H

Hall Of The Mountain King from Peer Gynt (Grieg)	TTL - Classical Collection
Have Yourself A Merry Little Christmas	TTL - Christmas Songs
How Do I Live	TTL - 90s Hits
	STL - Chart Hits

I

I Don't Want To Miss A Thing	TTL - 90s Hits
	TTL - Movie Hits
I Will Always Love You	TTL - Movie Hits
	TTL - Number One Hits
I'll Be There For You (Theme from Friends)	TTL - 90s Hits
	TTL - TV Themes
I've Got A Gal In Kalamazoo	TTL - Swing
In The Mood	TTL - Swing
It Don't Mean A Thing (If It Ain't Got That Swing)	TTL - Swing

J

Jailhouse Rock	TTL - Rock 'n' Roll
Jersey Bounce	TTL - Swing

L

La Bamba	TTL - Latin
La Isla Bonita	TTL - Latin
Let's Twist Again	TTL - Rock 'n' Roll
Little Donkey	TTL - Christmas Songs
Livin' La Vida Loca	TTL - Number One Hits
	TTL - Latin
Love's Got A Hold On My Heart	STL - Chart Hits

M

Match Of The Day	TTL - TV Themes
(Meet) The Flintstones	TTL - TV Themes
Men Behaving Badly	TTL - TV Themes
Minnie The Moocher	TTL - The Blues Brothers
Misty	TTL - Jazz
More Than Words	STL - Chart Hits
My Funny Valentine	TTL - Jazz
My Heart Will Go On	TTL - 90s Hits
	STL - Chart Hits

O

Old Landmark, The	TTL - The Blues Brothers
One O'Clock Jump	TTL - Jazz
Oye Mi Canto (Hear My Voice)	TTL - Latin

P

Peak Practice	TTL - TV Themes
Pennsylvania 6-5000	TTL - Swing
Polovtsian Dances from Prince Igor (Borodin)	TTL - Classical Collection

R

Radetzky March (Strauss)	TTL - Classical Collection
Rudolph The Red-Nosed Reindeer	TTL - Christmas Songs

S

Santa Claus Is Comin' To Town	TTL - Christmas Songs
Shake A Tail Feather	TTL - The Blues Brothers
She Caught The Katy And Left Me A Mule To Ride	TTL - The Blues Brothers
Sheep May Safely Graze (Bach)	TTL - Classical Collection
Simpsons, The	TTL - TV Themes
Sleigh Ride	TTL - Christmas Songs
Something About The Way You Look Tonight	TTL - 90s Hits
Soul Limbo	TTL - Latin
Star Wars (Main Theme)	TTL - Movie Hits
String Of Pearls, A	TTL - Swing
Summertime	TTL - Jazz
Swan, The from Carnival of the Animals (Saint-Säens)	TTL - Classical Collection
Sweet Home Chicago	TTL - The Blues Brothers
Symphony No. 40 in G Minor, 1st Movement (Mozart)	TTL - Classical Collection

T

Think	TTL - The Blues Brothers
Toreador's Song, The from Carmen (Bizet)	TTL - Classical Collection

W

When You Say Nothing At All	TTL - Number One Hits
	STL - Chart Hits
Wind Beneath My Wings, The	TTL - Movie Hits
Winter Wonderland	TTL - Christmas Songs

X

X-Files, The	TTL - TV Themes

Y

You Needed Me	TTL - Number One Hits
	STL - Chart Hits
You Can Leave Your Hat On	TTL - Movie Hits

Here's what you get with each book...

Take The Lead

90s Hits
Air That I Breathe - I'll Be There For You - Something About The Way You Look Tonight - Frozen - How Do I Live - Angels - My Heart Will Go On - I Don't Want To Miss A Thing

Movie Hits
Because You Loved Me, Blue Monday, (Everything I Do) I Do It For You, I Don't Want To Miss A Thing, I Will Always Love You, Star Wars, The Wind Beneath My Wings

TV Themes
Coronation Street, I'll Be There For You (Theme from Friends), Match Of The Day, (Meet) The Flintstones, Men Behaving Badly, Peak Practice, The Simpsons, The X-Files

The Blues Brothers
She Caught The Katy And Left Me A Mule To Ride - Gimme Some Lovin' - Shake A Tail Feather - Everybody Needs Somebody To Love - The Old Landmark - Think - Minnie The Moocher - Sweet Home Chicago

Christmas Songs
Winter Wonderland - Little Donkey - Frosty The Snowman - Rudolph The Red Nosed Reindeer - Christmas Song (Chestnuts Roasting On An Open Fire) - Have Yourself A Merry Little Christmas - Santa Claus Is Comin' To Town - Sleigh Ride

Swing
Chattanooga Choo Choo - Choo Choo Ch'Boogie - I've Got A Gal In Kalamazoo - In The Mood - It Don't Mean A Thing (If It Ain't Got That Swing) - Jersey Bounce - Pennsylvania 6-5000 - A String Of Pearls

Jazz
Birdland - Desafinado - Don't Get Around Much Anymore - Fascinating Rhythm - Misty - My Funny Valentine - One O'Clock Jump - Summertime

Latin
Bailamos - Cherry Pink And Apple Blossom White - Desafinado - Guantanamera - La Bamba - La Isla Bonita - Oye Mi Canto (Hear My Voice) - Soul Limbo

Number One Hits
Believe, Cher - Careless Whisper, George Michael - Dancing Queen, Abba - Flying Without Wings, Westlife - I Will Always Love You, Whitney Houston - Livin' La Vida Loca, Ricky Martin - When You Say Nothing At All, Ronan Keating - You Needed Me, Boyzone

Classical Collection
Sheep May Safely Graze (Bach) - Symphony No. 40 in G Minor, 1st Movement (Mozart) - The Toreador's Song from Carmen (Bizet) - Hall Of The Mountain King from Peer Gynt (Grieg) - Radetzky March (Strauss) - Dance Of The Sugar Plum Fairy from The Nutcracker (Tchaikovsky) - Polovtsian Dances from Prince Igor (Borodin) - The Swan from Carnival of the Animals (Saint-Säens)

Rock 'n' Roll
Be-Bop-A-Lula - Blue Suede Shoes - Blueberry Hill - C'mon Everybody - Great Balls Of Fire - The Green Door - Jailhouse Rock - Let's Twist Again

Share The Lead

Chart Hits
Dancing Queen - Flying Without Wings - How Do I Live - Love's Got A Hold On My Heart - My Heart Will Go On - More Than Words - When You Say Nothing At All - You Needed Me

Whatever your instrument is... you can

TAKE THE LEAD

Available for Violin
7240A	Swing
7177A	Jazz
7084A	The Blues Brothers
7025A	Christmas Songs
7006A	TV Themes
6912A	Movie Hits
6728A	90's Hits
7263A	Latin
7313A	Number One Hits
7508A	Classical Collection
7715A	Rock 'n' Roll

Available for Clarinet
7173A	Jazz
7236A	Swing
7080A	The Blues Brothers
7023A	Christmas Songs
7004A	TV Themes
6909A	Movie Hits
6726A	90's Hits
7260A	Latin
7309A	Number One Hits
7505A	Classical Collection
7711A	Rock 'n' Roll

Available for Drums
7179A	Jazz
7027A	Christmas Songs

Available for Trumpet
7083A	The Blues Brothers
7239A	Swing
7176A	Jazz
7262A	Latin
7312A	Number One Hits
7503A	Christmas Songs
7507A	Classical Collection
7714A	Rock 'n' Roll

Available for Tenor Saxophone
6911A	Movie Hits
7238A	Swing
7175A	Jazz
7082A	The Blues Brothers
7311A	Number One Hits
7637A	Christmas Songs
7713A	Rock 'n' Roll

Available for Piano
7178A	Jazz
7026A	Christmas Songs
7364A	Latin
7441A	Number One Hits
7509A	Classical Collection
7716A	Rock 'n' Roll

Available for Flute
6725A	90's Hits
7079A	The Blues Brothers
7235A	Swing
7172A	Jazz
7022A	Christmas Songs
7003A	TV Themes
6908A	Movie Hits
7259A	Latin
7310A	Number One Hits
7504A	Classical Collection
7710A	Rock 'n' Roll

Available for Alto Saxophone
7005A	TV Themes
7237A	Swing
7174A	Jazz
7081A	The Blues Brothers
7024A	Christmas Songs
6910A	Movie Hits
6727A	90's Hits
7261A	Latin
7308A	Number One Hits
7506A	Classical Collection
7712A	Rock 'n' Roll

COMING SOON...
Take The Lead *Grease*
Take The Lead *Ballads*
Share The Lead *TV / Film*

Available from:

Published by:
International Music Publications Ltd
Griffin House
161 Hammersmith Road
London
England W6 8BS

IMP

International
MUSIC
Publications

Registered In England No. 2703274
A Warner Music Group Company

Demonstration   Backing

The Green Door

Words by Marvin Moore
Music by Bob Davie

Jailhouse Rock

Words and Music by
Jerry Leiber and Mike Stoller

Demonstration   Backing

Let's Twist Again

Words and Music by
Kal Mann and David Appell

Bright pop (even 8's) ♩ = 160

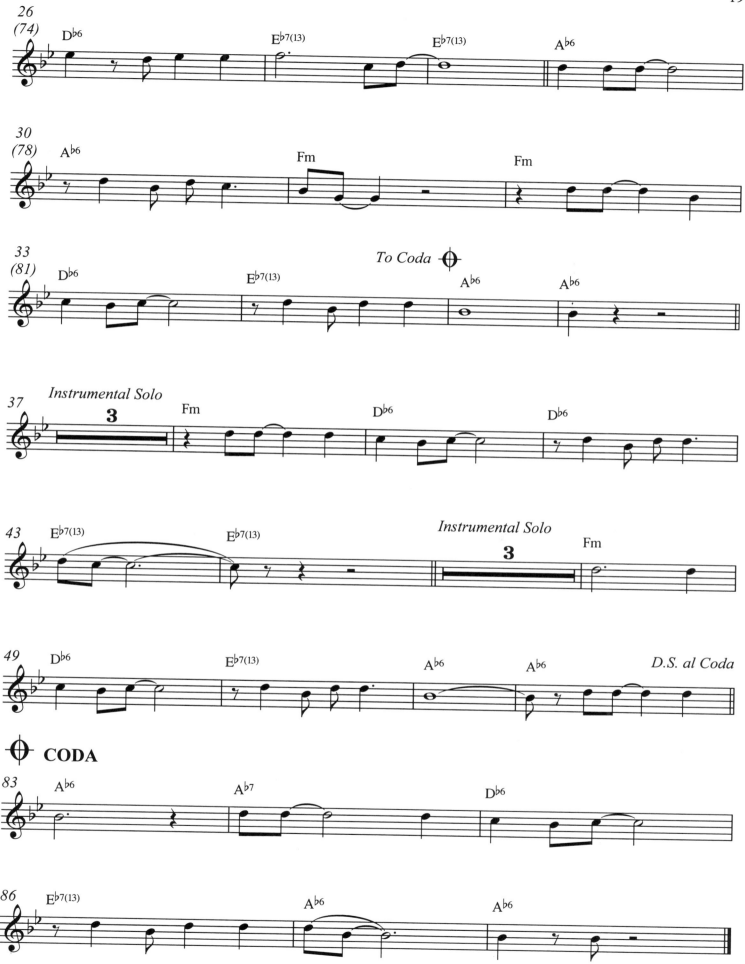